Poems to See Me Through

Janice Lawson

Front cover photo by D. Warren
Back cover photo by C. Boisvert

For Ed

Most of the poems in this collection were written long before you came into my world, but now you've become the poetry of my life.

TABLE OF CONTENTS

Prologue

After a few of my new, though nevertheless, quite dear friends showed interest in some of my long buried poetry, I began to search out, dig through, and reread them myself. I realized a certain amount of hypocrisy in the fact that I had been encouraging my friends to publish, while in fact, much of my own work had never seen the light of day. Or, at least, not for many years.

I did briefly consider the possibility that I could fold my poems neatly, wrap them in ribbon, and hide them in a dresser drawer for my friends and family to find upon my death, rushing the treasured bundles to the nearest publisher posthaste. However, I'm no Emily Dickinson, and my loved ones might already have full enough lives, that they would be more inclined to head to the recycling bin, than they would be sharing my whimsies and confessions with the world. I couldn't bear that eventuality.

So here they are, my little songs. I threw samples of just about everything in, the silliest, the saddest, the celebrations, even some so personal, I had a hard time opening them to the world. These are selections from decades of my life and years of writing, and include a few previously published under my earlier married name, Janice Allison. Hopefully, you will find one or two that will be meaningful, something to take away from these pages, maybe even a new idea to *see you through*.

So, "Come sit with me and let me sing..."

Sit With Me

Come sit with me and let me sing

A quiet song to you.

I'll stir some memories in your heart

And find some secrets, too.

Take a minute from your day.

Just rest with me awhile.

I'll touch some moments in your life.

I'll soothe and make you smile.

I'll ease the tensions from your mind,

Establish some rapport.

Relax yourself; I'll do the work.

That's what a poet's for.

REFLECTIONS

Time to Go

I would like to leave this place

To blaze a swath, my own frontier,

To let this hungry heart of mine

Embrace a n'er seen sphere.

I've used it up, 'tis vacuum.

My friends have empty eyes.

I think my life has moved away

And left me this disguise.

Fleeting Thoughts of an Encore

It happens rarely now,

But what a thrill when a glimmer of the old me

Shines and flutters about the new mundane me.

Oh, she was something.

Full of life and creative as spring.

Sometimes, when I read her words,

I am breathless with awe.

How wonderful that she didn't know about life.

She only believed in it.

That is where true inspiration gives rise.

Long before the cynicism

And regret pervades the soul,

And chokes the heart,

There is devout belief in

Life.

I wonder…

No, too late, too late.

Janice Lawson

Moving Day

On a winter bleak December day

A hope filled dream was proved.

We packed and stacked, and treasures sacked,

And despite mere blizzard, moved.

My love a home had built for me

Long nights and stolen hours.

Unfinished true, but warm and stout,

This simple shell was ours.

We settled in on plywood floors

'neath windows spattered thick

From drywall spray adorning

Wherever such might stick.

The foil-backed insulation gleamed

Through studs laid barren yet,

And doors not hung like soldiers stood

About the walls stained wet.

Lights, too, we had, but hung awry,

Nor tops our counters fine.

But there amid the cartons high,

The joy this house was mine.

The dreams we shared for carpet, drapes,

Those, too, I knew would come

As paneled walls and closet rods

Appeared there one by one.

And in that incompleted state

I knew we couldn't fail.

For hope had raised these very walls

While love drove every nail.

And with that thought, I viewed the mess,

And smiled, 'cause life's that way.

That house would never look as grand

As it did on moving day.

Inspired by Ree and Kent Christensen

The House

I thought of him today,

My once and former spouse.

Because a callous twist of fate

Led me past our house.

All these years avoiding ghosts

I thought we'd left behind

To lurk the cottage love had built,

Not one there could I find.

The memories and cherished hopes,

The bitter-lived despair

I thought we'd left about the place

Weren't there. They just weren't there.

I realize now they're in my heart,

Those memories we started.

And the black despair ceased to be

The very day we parted.

And saddest yet, those cherished hopes

Were only mine alone.

They're what I used to start again.

How foolish I'd not known.

My dreams of happiness, not there,

For I've found love since then.

Those ghosts that haunt the past, benign,

Locked here inside they've been.

Whatever it was we thought we had,

That house of ours just told it.

It wasn't worth the keeping,

So we split it up and sold it.

Photo by C. Boisvert

Winter Wind

Touch me softly, winter wind.

Caress me now so kindly.

Cool the flush that stings my face.

Dry the tears that blind me.

Wrap me in your icy grasp.

Numb me with your spray.

Tranquilize this burning rage,

And take my pain away.

Two angry hearts have clashed and sparked,

Their kinship torn asunder.

Transport me that I might forget

How senseless was my blunder.

Too many words are spoke in haste

To salve our discontent.

And now to save my arrogant pride,

I've said words I never meant.

Animosity breeds no growing thing.

I've nothing to defend,

Just the horrid thought, could be

I've lost a cherished friend.

So touch me softly, winter wind,

Desensitize my sorrow.

Tonight I need your soothing chill

To face myself tomorrow.

Photo by D. Warren

A Quiet Place

Every person needs a quiet place, a humble hideaway,

A place for introspection, where pretense falls away.

Every person needs a mountain top, time alone to be apart

To cleanse the burdens from his soul, the secrets from his heart.

Every person needs a chapel, a quiet place to pray,

A place to plan tomorrow, a place to end today.

Every person needs a moment to turn inside his own

And face the tender stirrings that only he has known.

Grandma's Chinaberry Tree

My grandma had a chinaberry tree

With one low sprawling branch

That beckoned me to swing aloft

With every stolen chance.

I'd ride the wind with china fruit

Bouncing in my hair,

And view the world's diminished size,

Enthroned upon the air.

It afforded me a vantage spot

Where life fell into place,

And fortified again I'd climb

Back down from outer space.

Now Grandma's gone, and too, her tree,

But in my yard, a willow

Where my child ascends the wind

To sail transfixed its billow.

Now when my life outgrows its bounds

And my composure's in the lurch,

I yearn to climb above it all

With that willow for my perch.

But convention dictates I'm too old,

And it's not the same, I know

As Grandma's chinaberry was

Those few short years ago.

But I wonder watching her up there

If ever there will be

A simpler way to look at life

Than borne astride a tree.

Illusion

Her smiles are all for him they say.

Such devotion is inspired.

A perfect couple, happily wed

And universally admired.

They watch her hand upon his sleeve,

His kiss upon her brow.

A love so publicly displayed

Is rare these days of now.

And when apart she speaks of him

In terms that fairly glow,

He'll not stay long. He'll rush right home

To be at her side, they know.

Two common people sharing love

Of such uncommon scope

Provokes a subtle envious awe

And fills our lives with hope.

They appreciate each other.

It's evident they care

And regard the other with respect.

So what secret do they share?

What driving need has brought them close?

How is it she can see

Every whim and thought and trait

Of his, a quality?

Would their friends, their fans be shocked;

Would truth their envy smother

To learn the secret these two share

Is that she loves another?

Untitled

There is in your smile a reckless notion

That life is not such a serious thing,

And just maybe, no matter what,

Everything will work out....

It gives me courage to do many things.

Little Hearts

Photo by D. Warren

Preschool Teachers

Preschool teachers have their pleasures,

Dewey kisses and sticky treasures,

Desperate hugs and runny noses,

Memories of tedious poses,

Grateful smile, the splinter's gone,

Serene silence, day is done,

Safe retrieve from atop the slide,

Juice moustaches, grape and wide,

Peanut butter and spilled milk,

Tiny "thank you's," soft as silk,

Off-key voices, heralding hope,

Not enough water, too much soap,

Friendships made, little hearts broken,

Reality learned, fantasy spoken,

Long on color, short on style,

An all-consuming four-inch smile,

Rested mothers, fortified kids,

Playhouse drama, misplaced lids,

Non-stop needs, eager faces,

Stories about far-off places,

Poster paint, wooden block castles,

Dress up clothes with pompom tassels,

Not enough money, too little time,

Total fulfillment, reward sublime.

Published in Mother's Manual, July, 1977

But First

Why don't you lift that heavy hand?

Don't push him quite so much.

He'll respond more certainly

To your simple loving touch.

Give him a chance to be himself

With confidence and pride.

Let him know you're always there,

Not behind, but at his side.

Guide, but don't restrict his growth.

Broaden his awareness.

Smile at him, and if you must,

Judge his work with fairness.

Don't make mistakes that many do,

Thinking people start out bad,

And only through our constant drilling

Goodness can be had.

He's just a tiny lump of clay

With life dumped all about him.

He's got to touch and taste his world

And witness traits to have them.

His consciousness grows every day,

Blithely gathering samples,

So fill his senses with great things.

Throw him some examples.

I hope he can attain your goals,

Fulfill the plans you've styled.

But he has to have a little time

For being first, a child.

Presented during 1979 International Year of the Child celebrations, Church of the Eternal Hills, Grand Lake, Colorado,   King of Glory Lutheran Church, Denver

Love's Enough

I am a teacher of children.

Sometimes when then come to me,

Tearful at having left their mothers,

And frightful of who I might be,

Whoever I might be,

I don't know what to do for them.

There's a hesitant frightfulness in me, too,

That I might not be able to give this tiny person

Anything of value, and

This vital year will be wasted.

But when I take the trembling child onto my lap,

And he sobs into my heart,

And begins to trust the security of my compassion,

I begin to love him,

And offtimes,

Love's enough.

School Should Start

Children zooming,

Tension blooming,

Families rooming,

Limited space.

Children screaming,

Summer steaming,

Mother dreaming

A quiet place.

Sonny loping,

Sister moping,

Mother hoping

Strife depart.

Bedlam growing,

Boredom showing

Mother knowing

School should start!

Someone Special

Great power there within her hands

To foster growth and learning,

To fulfill what was only dream,

Satisfy a yearning.

Her approval deems a scribble

Some precious work of art.

Her healing touch can numb the pain

Or mend a broken heart.

Her encouragement gives significance

To even the simplest stride,

Assures victory, saves the day,

Implements trust and pride.

She is surely someone special,

Life's answer to all things.

Empress with a magic wand,

Great wisdom from her springs.

How respected her dominion,

So reverent her post,

Her failure would destroy the world

For the person she loves most.

But she can calm the frenzied soul

And warm the chillest gloom,

Create a fairyland affair,

Enlighten any room.

Her helping hand insures success.

She's powers like no other.

Her command ordained by God

For she's become a mother.

Masterpiece

The easel stood between us.

She worked on the other side.

All I could see was legs and feet

And paint that dripped and dried.

I stopped what I was doing,

And a smile replaced my frown

Because there's much about a child

To see from two knees down,

A bandaid and a shin bruise,

The hem of a painting shirt,

Oxfords needing polish,

Tense knees, wet paint, and dirt.

One shoestring lay in a pool of paint,

The other, a hopeless knot.

A masterpiece was growing there,

The painting and the tot.

Previously published in The Lyric, 1979, Sky-Hi News, 1979

Reprise

I'd raise my kids much differently

Could I do it all over again.

I'd say, "We can't do any chores today!"

"We've worthier tasks," I'd proclaim, and then...

"Grab your treasure buckets and forest boots!

We must search the dark and dapply wood

For magic pinecones and ginger-colored twigs."

That's how I'd re-raise my kids if I could.

I wouldn't require so many naps,

Blessed with the wisdom that I have now.

We'd spend the time cooking adventurous feasts

Of wizard's wink soup and funny stuff chow.

And bathing's merely redundant, I'm sure.

We won't fight anymore about it.

But run through sprinklers in our ' jama tops,

And who's to know when we've done without it.

We'd write our friends songs if they'd care to dance,

Compose tales of our wiliest days.

We'd move to the library to live in the poems,

And travel more trips and audience more plays.

When I'm exhausted, weakened, and weary

From this marathon pace we are on,

I'll rise like the phoenix with hindsight to guide me,

Remembering how quickly these fledglings are gone.

It's really too bad that you can't start anew.

Parenting without practice was rough.

But I'll be one truly fine grandma,

If (and whenever) I get old enough.

Piano Practice

The sour sounds of plodding plinks,

Chordless rhythm rise and sinks.

Hesitating faltered pause,

Concentration for the cause.

Over and again the sound

Until the proper note is found.

Auditory grief each day.

Did Mozart's mom despair this way?

Previously published in Olympus by Mile High Poetry Society, 1993

Little Slow-Poke

Little slow-poke, there you are

Wishing on another star,

You've no shoes or stockings on,

But then, who cares, the bus has gone.

What am I to do with you,

Smiling off into the blue,

Dancing now before the glass?

You'll break my heart, you impish lass.

I hate to burst into your dreams,

But you're late to school again, it seems.

Teddy Bear

The preschool class was over.

The children each had gone.

The room now echoed silence,

And I was all alone.

I closed and locked the windows

And bolted fast the door,

Then began retrieving toys

Strewn about the floor.

It was only then I saw him,

Forgotten and forlorn,

A teddy bear amid the mess,

Faded, loved, and worn.

He wasn't one of our toys,

Although, I wished t'was true.

He belonged to someone special,

Though I couldn't figure who.

I lifted him and felt the life

That only love can bring

When a tiny person gives his heart

To a fluffy treasured thing.

I studied that amazing bear,

A bedraggled little guy.

I think he once was yellow,

And of course, had but one eye.

I placed him gently on the shelf

With another bear,

But, oh, it wrenched my heart to see

How lonely he looked there.

I wanted to call someone,

But I couldn't figure who.

Tonight someone I loved a lot

Would sleep without his Pooh.

Because You're You

Little child with eyes asparkle,

Absorbing all this wonder,

How beautifully you touch my world,

How soft, with love, what thunder!

Racing through my life unchecked,

Stirring my emotions.

Concentrating, but not long,

Sweet head, a school of notions.

Before society harnesses

Your shocking honest air,

Teach me more about yourself.

What pixie lives in there?

Precious sapling, what I'd give

To make your dreams come true.

Your mother loves you 'cause you're hers,

And I, because you're you.

Presented during 1979 International Year of the Child celebrations, Church of the Eternal Hills, Grand Lake, Colorado   King of Glory Lutheran Church, Denver, Colorado

Sprite

Her entrance was a litheful dash.

She boarded with a jump.

And a squirming sway for balance

Commenced the tedious pump.

Her system worked, and it began

To lift her toward the blue,

With honey hair to tag behind

The perfect arc she flew.

Rapid ascent to the heavens,

Peak, and retrace to the ground,

Continuous full semi-circle,

Back again, and around.

The moment held its own beauty

Of a graceful, moving thing,

A permanence in my memory,

A sprite upon a swing.

THE LAND I LOVE

Photo by D.H. Leonhardt

Pewter Morning

Gleaming out my window

Pewter morning on the park.

Black mountains heave immenseness,

Emerging from the dark.

Fog ending just below the clouds.

Where's the sun? Not here.

Loneliness, but peaceful,

Wet things everywhere.

Ghosty whispers sailing by,

Rooftops blowing smoke,

Silver streets awaiting use,

And not a sound is spoke.

Wait, there is someone, a car

Creeping, splattering the still,

Autographing parallels.

It mars the gleam at will.

Now there are others, and my own

Anticipating day.

It may not look this way again,

But neither it nor I may stay.

Previously published in the Sky-Hi News, Granby, Colorado

Hear the Music

There's a concert in the mountains

Held this time each fall,

An opera of color change,

Promised to enthrall.

So come enjoy the spectacle,

Taste the fragrance tart,

But this year don't miss the music.

Listen with your heart.

The evergreens provide the bass,

Humming in the wind,

The blue sky, velvet harmony.

Symphony begin!

The prelude now proceeds to flow,

Rhapsody of gold.

Each section is a different shade

Lime to scarlet bold.

The orchestra performs its work

As each color plays.

Apricot tones are round and smooth,

Amber simply sways.

Reds are haunting sounds of horns,

Brilliant copper, crimson,

Yellow trumpets, and a flute,

Iridescent lemon.

When a hillside is emblazoned,

Music thunders, then

The next scene is more evergreen, the

Music's soft again.

Harps are honey-colored foliage,

Staccato notes, flame.

You think there's only silence there?

I hear it just the same.

And as the symphony rising,

Makes its final sound,

The leaves now spent, conclude and fall,

Exhausted to the ground.

Previously published in Parnassus by Mile-Hi Poetry Society, 1991

The Horses

They flew, undulating grace

Striping earth-sprung colors

Across my vision.

Wild eyes leading rhythms

Of body and wind through

The morning's frost.

I would have abandoned vehicle

To leap astride, equestrian,

And share the thrill.

But the cowboy closed the gate

And they were gone.

Photo by D.H. Leonhardt

September Star

Eight years I've watched the colors change,

Eight autumns in these mountains,

Watched in awe the hills erupt in

Shimmering gold fountains.

And though each breathtaking season

Is as stunning as the rest,

I anticipate the turning

Of one tree that's always best.

For this frail and quakie aspen,

Unobtrusive until fall,

Stands there unnoticed summer long,

Then quite amazes all.

As if on cue the scene ignites.

Each from green to golden turns,

But this inconsequential quake

A fiery copper burns.

A rusty crimson superstar

With brilliant pigmentation,

Pales its gold compatriots with

Flaming exaltation.

I think in life that's how we are,

Compliant with conformance

Until our chance to step out front

And give our best performance.

So, once again with faith I watch.

For this latent star I wait.

He'll steal the show again I know,

September's potentate.

Previously published in Grand County Heritage Cook Book, 1979

Photo by B. Lawson

Colorado Centennial

On the eve of the state centennial

We planned to celebrate

One hundred years of statehood,

A conquered land still great.

We'd built our home upon her breast

And littered on her brow.

We'd mocked and marred her grandeur,

Domesticated now.

A land of skyscraping barriers,

Unrelenting bitter cold,

But her majesty was ours at last.

We'd stripped her of her gold.

The statewide celebration

The morning soon would bring.

We'd conquered the unconquerable,

But the rains would ruin this thing.

Already now they had begun.

From the very crown it streamed,

An apocalyptic monster

Befalling us it seemed.

It grew and flew, rushing through

The gullies and ravines,

A flooding mass of nature's wrath,

Of thundering machines.

It ravaged Big Thompson Canyon,

Each figment of our creation,

Swallowed and regurgitated,

Abyss of desecration.

One hundred eighty people dead.

Happy Birthday, Mile-High State.

It's not the taming of the earth

That we should celebrate.

For here in the purple darkness

Of Long's Peak's angry shade,

In this shadow it all began,

And here our state was made.

And on its head the first drop fell,

A torrential reprimand.

One hundred years we've been a state,

But never ours, the land.

Monument

Mankind has engineered

Architectural confections,

Monoliths of structured steel,

Monumental stone erections.

But never beauty, strength,

Nor statuesquely grand a thing

As the tiny crocus through the snow

To face the sky in spring.

Previously published in Grand County Heritage Cookbook, 1979

Lulu City, 1879-1883

Where the trail climbed to timberline

And the Never Summers loomed,

Just beneath the great divide,

Lulu City boomed.

Four avenues and nineteen streets

Formed a hundred city blocks

Where structures sprang like topsy,

And miners hailed in flocks

To patronize Godsmark's Hotel,

Buy provisions at his store,

Frequent Halley's fine saloon,

And prospect silver ore.

Two lumber mills attested hope

Prosperity's about.

Five hundred residents poured in,

And then the ore ran out.

How quickly time forgets its own

As nature repossesses.

Lulu's now a paragraph

The history book addresses.

"Lulu was never of consequence,"

Perhaps the record's true.

But silver was king, she it's queen

In 1882.

"Lulu City" was first published in Grand County Heritage Cookbook in 1979, and later integrated into the five area pageants presented in celebration of Rocky Mountain National Park's Diamond Jubilee, 1990 (which also appears later in this collection).

Historically I am probably not accurate with my line, "the ore ran out." It is more widely believed Lulu's residents abandoned their mines when the decision was made to run the railroad line through Granby 16 miles to the south, rather than through Grand Lake, which would have afforded a more practical and economical way to transport the ore out of the mountains.

Rocky Mountain National Park still maintains the hiking trail to what little remains of Lulu City today.

America Sings

America sings of treasured things,

Of educated masses,

Of wilderness and enterprise,

Of wealth and prairie grasses.

America sings in special ways,

Bar mitzvahs and communions,

With rodeos and barbecues

And family reunions.

America sings in subtle tones

In understated places,

With calloused hands and brotherhood,

Through tears and children's faces.

America sings and freedom rings

For peoples who have come

To build a nation's majesty

And simply call it home.

Published in Grand County Heritage Cookbook 1979

HYMNS OF FAITH

The Old Log Church

*Written in celebration as the church found its new and permanent home in City
Park, Granby, Colorado*

What lives have touched these chapel doors?

And knelt inside to pray?

How many in these fifty years

Have stopped here on their way?

And little church, what hope gave you

Nomadic heads bent low,

A fortress in the hardest times,

A shrine upon the snow?

How many hearts were joined in one

Within this rustic hall?

How many found his presence here

Behind your weathered wall?

And did your humble bosom swell,

Tender treasures within ring

With joyful aspirations here,

And hearty praises sing?

How like a temple you've become

To bless a thousand fold.

May God bestow his smile on thee.

These walls his grace uphold.

Published in Grand County Heritage Cookbook, 1979

Photo by B. Lawson

Christmas Cactus

Truth there is in gentle boast

That simple things are treasured most.

This Christmas gaily fostered joy

In welcome home and Santa's toy,

With fellowship for brotherhood,

An evergreen festooned there stood.

The gifts of love and memories old,

While Christmas first again we told.

But none of these as warm the sight

As the joy I found on Christmas night

When kneeling in that darkened room.

My Christmas cactus wore a bloom!

Stashed away to dormant sleep,

Forgotten there, its secret keep.

While festive moments caroled on

This humble plant observed alone

The age old miracle of birth

That touches every life on earth.

But nothing ever touched me so

As learning even cactus know.

Pond Lily

I'm as the fragile lily pad

Whose softly drifting mass

Adorns her world with tempered calm

And floats the surface glass,

And though the tempests toss her, will

In lurching gale not die,

For when the storm subsides, she's there,

Still glistening at the sky.

So beautiful, that tender strength

To endure as lilies do,

Riding ripples in life's wake,

Lone isle upon the blue.

But had you stood upon the rock

And watched her from the shore,

And had the sun from out the cloud

Illuminated more,

You'd seen in bright revealing ray

The truth uncovered shows

Deep from the earth beneath the pond

The stalwart stem that grows,

A lifeline to the surface fast,

The lily holding tight,

And even in the fiercest gust,

Supported by its might.

For the lily isn't water borne,

But from the mud has sprung,

And through the airless depths she grew,

From earth to life was flung.

And so I am, from earth to air

Uplifted by the stem

Of God's supporting arm held fast,

Afloat, but strong in Him.

Inspired by the gift of a photograph by Linda Pepler

Hummingbird

I held a hummingbird in my hand

And grieved the lifeless thing,

But marveled at the rainbowed gloss

Still brilliant on his wing.

Iridescently the sun's caress

Shimmering the gem,

Glittered greens and ruby throat

The tiny length of him.

I prayed to God this death in error,

The deed be now undone.

And peering wistfully I saw

His eye. He opened one.

Trembling, awed at all great things,

I raised my treasure to the sky.

And with new wisdom knew respect.

Through tears I watched him fly.

He Won't Leave You There

When you think you've lost it all

And life's a bottomless abyss,

There's simply nowhere else to turn,

Just remember this.

There's a God who planned our destiny,

Created us with care,

Who watches tediously our plight.

He won't leave you there.

For some ethereal reason

This whole grand scheme was plotted

With roles and accountabilities

To each of us allotted.

If this Master of existence

Maneuvers animation,

Imagine what's in store for you,

His pinnacle of creation.

So thank Him for this test of strength.

Serve His purpose, great or small,

For you're important here or else

You'd not be here at all.

Without You

I've tried to imagine a world without flowers,

A drab, dismal void of colorless hours,

Or fathom a life with no music to hear,

Joyless and cheerless, and boring, I fear.

I've tried to imagine my world without light,

No sunsets or mornings and meaningless sight.

I've conjured vast deserts because there's no rain,

Supposed without friendship we'd each be insane.

I tried to imagine my world without you,

But the pain of the thought diminished the view.

The treasures of life grew increasingly small,

Until, without you, life was nothing at all.

Silly Songs

Texas Twang

After years of formal education

I improved my speech.

I moved away and (rue the day)

Put that dialect from my reach.

My pronunciation is superb.

My diction is divine,

And I lament there's no accent,

No twang left to refine.

But, oh, how the situation changes

When Texans come to call.

From way down south I find my mouth

And I out-drawl 'em all.

So there's just no point in denying

Those roots from whence ya' sprang.

Though I may roam, I'm still at home

With a good old Texas twang.

Photo by S. Warren

Snow is great stuff

If you've got a sled,

And being snowed in

Is all in your head.

You can get out and

Make statues and things,

Roll, and fall down,

And flap big angel wings.

'Cuz if you like trouncing

And being real cold,

Snow is great stuff and

You're never too old.

The Snowmobiler

An imposing figure on the snow,

He glides with ease across the plain.

Black panther racing through the cloud

Of crystals. He banks, and back again.

An athlete muscling his machine,

Powering up the steepest hill,

Flinging his weight to make the drop

At breakneck speeds just for the thrill.

My hero, he. My idol, him,

Zooming past with ne'r a glance.

Carving tracks 'cross each fresh snow,

With every given chance.

Then mindless of the dangers there,

Into the forest dense he steers,

And finds the deepest, darkest hole,

To sink from sight up to his ears!

Dilemma

A syncopated melody lullaby's my brain.

Enchanting words enunciate, create a new refrain.

Stanzas born and verses grow until the urge has won.

But how can I write poetry when laundry's to be done?

Today's a proper time for diminishing this pile

Of aromatic socks and togs strewn about the tile.

But organizing syllables are rippling off my tongue.

Now should one play at poetry when laundry's to be done?

Ah, Mother English cleverly controlled's a vicious vice.

The sinful lengths I'd go to hear those jingling sounds ring twice.

Uncalculated times this game has kept me up the night.

Could justice do I perma-press? There's poetry to write!

Irony

What irony lies in the fact

Dare I judge, criticize, rant, or rail,

Life presents me immediately

The chance to show how, and I fail.

Football Season

Fall hath fell

And football season hath arriven.

He sits all day before the tube

While up the wall I'm driven.

I'm off-sides if I dare to walk

In front of the TV set,

And the penalty if I try to talk,

Unsportsmanlike conduct, yet.

"Tis for his health I worry most,

The ranting and the raving.

The man is fairly glassy-eyed,

Stamping feet and arms awaving.

So, if your man is acting strangely,

Believe me, there is reason.

It's a nation-wide epidemic...

Football season.

Published in Sky-Hi News when I wrote the Grand Lake News, early 1970's

U.S.P.O.

I love to go to the post office.

Such joy in getting mail!

A postcard announcing my catalog's come

Cheers me without fail.

Junkmail, cards, and special offers,

A letter from a friend,

Even a bill is proof I'm worth

The time it took to send.

The only thing that annoys me so

I can hardly bear and grin it

Is to stick my nose inside the box

And find there's nothing in it.

Box of Love

Christmas is a precious time

To each of us, it's true

One reason is traditions

We've grown accustomed to.

Now, take this one for instance,

Both Mom and I, the same,

We both are box and ribbon savers.

Recycle is our game.

It's gotten so through all these years

Some have held up well.

We've passed the same box back and forth

More times than I can tell.

Now, I can't quite remember

What she gave me this last year,

But I know t'was in that yellow box

I've come to hold so dear.

Surely, it was '92

I gave that box to Dad

And put on top that old green bow

Our family's always had.

Well, we've plenty of traditions

We've treasured down through time,

And I'll bet your family's

Are 'bout as quaint as mine.

But, you know there's something warm

And nostalgic, don't you see,

In placing that same box of love

Each year beneath our tree.

The Grand Lake Pageant

Photo by D.H.Leonhardt

ACT IV "The Park"

The Grand Lake Pageant—ACT IV

"The Park"

When Rocky Mountain National Park was established in 1915, the tiny community of Grand Lake, Colorado, guardians of The Park's West Gate, celebrated. Included in the festivities was a choral reading written by Mary Lyons Cairns about the first inhabitants of the area. Her poetry, "The Indians," was to become Act I of the Grand Lake Pageant, when in 1940, at the Silver Anniversary of the Park's existence, Carolyn Rhone added Act II to celebrate "The Settlers." Caroline Holzwarth then added the third act in 1965 to honor "The Miners," and the Golden Anniversary.

Happily, my mother, Hope Lawson and I, were challenged to create a fourth act for the Diamond Jubilee in 1990. Our subject was to be "The Park," while keeping the Victorian style of the earlier works. Mother, a local newspaper columnist, helped with research and editing, while I, by then a published poet, wrote the verse. The entire pageant of four acts, was then performed five times that summer in local venues.

As the only surviving contributing poet, I look forward to enjoying the addition of Act V, in the summer of 2015, when Rocky will celebrate its centennial year. Here follows my work from 1990….

The Spirit of Shadow Mountain is replaced by the Spirit of the Park. (Voices) the chorus divides into two groups, East and West, Estes Park and Grand Lake. The Spirit is upstage between the divided choruses. Enos is downstage to address the audience. Isabella Bird, The Earl of Dunraven, Roger Toll, Horace Albright, and David Brower are part of the Estes Park chorus, (whose lines are their own words from their original publications). The Advocate is in the Grand Lake chorus.

Both choruses:

"Loveliness dwells here…in the land where the columbine grows."

Enos Mills:

Unbounded wealth where the columbine grows!

An untapped fortune for a man with dreams,

Timber, and meadows where cattle may graze.

We'll water the plains with these mountain streams.

Where others have failed, I will succeed.

Hunters will come as the miners before

To harvest the bighorn, the deer, and the elk,

The eagle and beaver, if not the ore.

In Long's Peak's shadow I'll build a home,

For all I survey is mine to possess.

Yes, unbounded wealth for a man with dreams.

I'll carve my fortune from this wilderness.

Earl of Dunraven:

> Run your cattle on these emerald hills.

> Stake your claim and make your stand.

> Lead your hunters to the craggy slopes.

> You've a vision, boy. We must own this land!

Enos:

> I will own this land!

The Spirit of the Park:

> Enos, you speak with the voice of your youth.

> This nation's wave of greed you impart.

> Your life's work won't be what you perceive,

> For one day you'll measure this land with your heart.

Enos:

> Mysterious Mother, how can you know me?

> My dreams are as sure as the lupine in Spring,

> As clear as the Poudre, Bear Lake and the sky,

> As vast as the glaciers and waters they bring.

Spirit:

> And like the glaciers, those dreams melt away.
>
> But a glacier first alters all in its path.
>
> So come, Enos, begin to know your true quest.
>
> Come study my beauty; come witness my wrath.

Enos:

> What voice says this? By what name are you known?

Spirit:

> Thousands of names from as many years,
>
> The Arapaho called me "the land between."
>
> Your people say, "one of the last frontiers."
>
> The spirit that calls from the mountains high,
>
> The song of the wind through the evergreens,
>
> The soaring eagle's cry.
>
> I am the land,
>
> The heart of the Rockies, the Great Divide,
>
> Where tundra skirts steepled citadels
>
> And the bighorn sheep abide.

I am the seasons

That sparkle like crystal in winter's cold

And burst from the bloom of a summer's green

To shimmering aspen's gold.

I am the fountain,

Annointed with clouds, bequeathed of the snow,

Mother of waters coursing a way

To the canyons below.

Enos:

And vain, are you not, of your power o'er Man?

But be well advised, he won't be denied.

You'll not spurn his coming. His conquest is sure

To plunder this treasure...

Enos and Spirit:

Believe me...

Spirit: (angrily)

...he's tried.

What faith have I in the words of men

Whose frantic resolutions wane

In the face of a raging mountain storm

Or a blinding blizzards's bane?

Need I but stir the wind a bit

To send them skittering to the plains?

Need I but clothe myself anew

To obliterate their sad remains?

What faith have I in boasts of might?

For I belong to no man's designs.

He will vanish from the earth

Ere my seasons change a hundred times.

Where are the valiant Arapaho, Ute,

Whom I sheltered, clothed, and fed?

Mighty warriors? Dust of my flesh!

Or from this land have fled.

Enos:

They fled in the face of the white man's climb

To mine these hills and rob your veins.

Those miners were a victorious lot.

Here is where the ambitious reigns.

Spirit:

> And where are they now, these miners you tout?
>
> Their "reign" was as brief as a day.
>
> For a moment they littered their rubbish about
>
> And as quickly they scurried away.

Grand Lake Chorus:

> Where the trail climbed to timberline
>
> And the Never Summers loomed,
>
> Just beneath the great divide,
>
> Lulu City boomed.
>
> Four avenues and nineteen streets
>
> Formed a hundred city blocks
>
> Where structures sprang like topsy,
>
> And miners hailed in flocks
>
> To patronize Godsmark's Hotel,
>
> Buy provisions at his store,
>
> Frequent Halley's fine saloon,
>
> And prospect silver ore.
>
> Two lumber mills attested hope
>
> Prosperity's about.

Five hundred residents poured in,

And then the ore ran out.

Spirit: (mockingly)

And then the "men" ran out.

Grand Lake Chorus:

How quickly time forgets its own

As nature repossesses.

Lulu's now a paragraph

The history book addresses.

Spirit:

Lulu was never of consequence.

Grand Lake Chorus:

Perhaps the record's true.

But silver was king, she it's queen

In 1882.

Enos:

Your judgement of men is harsh, and unfair,

While your gifts are abundant and free.

You have not denied your treasures abound.

Why will you not share them with me?

Spirit:

But I will, Enos! Don't misunderstand.

These gifts are for you and all men.

But first learn precisely what they are.

Take them then, and only then.

Enos:

You deny me to hunt the elk and the deer.

The eagle flies free from my gun.

The timber and ore you give not to me,

Yet the Utes you permitted each one.

Spirit:

The Utes knew the land, for the Mother am I.

They valued the gifts they beheld.

They exploited not with overuse.

In harmonious balance we dwelled.

Enos:

Then what did they know that I do not?

And what treasures do I not perceive

Why am I not yet worthy of you?

What more would you have me believe?

Isabella Bird:

"The scenery is the most glorious

I have ever seen,

And it is above us, around us,

At the very door.

Never to be forgotten glories they are."

Horace Albright:

"One of the most amazing vistas of mountains and forests

Ever given men the privilege of seeing."

Earl of Dunraven:

> "Everything is huge and stupendous.
>
> Nature is formed in a larger mould
>
> Full of vigor and young life.
>
> The air is scented with the sweet-smelling
>
> Sap of the pines."

Roger Toll:

> "Surely if one can ever grasp
>
> The infinity of time and space
>
> It is here, standing on the peak
>
> And looking off to the vanishing horizon."

Isabella:

> "I would not now exchange my memories
>
> Of its perfect beauty and extraordinary sublimity
>
> For any other experience in any other part of the world.
>
> This is surely one of the most entrancing spots on earth."

Spirit: (impassioned)

> The true legacy of the Rockies

Can't be measured in dollars or gold.

Look about you and wonder that the

Splendor you see is all your heart can hold.

The pristine beauty of a perfect land,

A breath of the purest air,

Memories of a fawn at play

Will follow you everywhere.

Stand on the crest of a snowy peak,

Touch a tundra flower bedewed.

Race with the wind on a rocky ridge

And come away renewed.

Follow the elk to an alpine glade,

Tread softly where the columbine grow.

Sleep on a fragrant forest floor,

And awake to the alpenglow.

This land is yours, not piece by piece,

But the whole of it, total and grand,

From tortured windswept timberline

To the gentle lodgepole's stand.

Make your peace with the mountain.

Of its towering strength be a part,

And take of its bounty only those things

You can carry away in your heart.

Both Choruses:

Take of its bounty only those things

You can carry away in your heart.

Spirit: (walks to stage exit, stops, and turns)

Build your cabin, Enos.

Rest in the shade of Long's Peak.

And when you can call a name for me,

All mankind will hear you speak.

(Spirit of the Park exits)

Both Choruses:

So the axe of young Enos rang in the wood,

And the voice of the Park in his ear.

The savage land he'd thought to tame

Was the Eden he'd come to revere.

He watched as cattle trampled meadows

Where once wildflowers grew.

He stood by as forests were stripped away

And he knew what he must do.

His destiny was hers; her future his.

Boyhood dreams were replaced with a goal.

He fought to save this wilderness

Ere expansion took its toll.

He wrote of her grandeur, preached of her worth,

Bade a changing nation observe;

Wilderness, once something to conquer,

Must now be a prize to preserve.

He turned the eyes of a nation

With respect, to a vanishing world.

Where the powers of nature still triumphed

The American flag unfurled.

Enos: (addressing Grand Lake Chorus)

"My youthful dream had been to scale peak after peak

And from the earthly spires to see the scenic

World far below and far away."

Advocate:

"Elsewhere man must live by the sweat of his brow.

Here let him rest and play."

Enos: (addressing Estes Park chorus)

"I wish that everyone might have a campfire

At Mother Nature's hearthstone.

A campfire in the forest marks the most

Enchanting place on life's highway

Wherein to have a lodging for the night.

David Brower:

"The wilderness we have now is all that we will ever have.'

Both Choruses:

"Conserve the scenery,

The natural and historic objects therein.

Leave them unimpaired for the enjoyment

Of future generations."

Enos: (addressing the audience)

"People need the temples of the Gods,

The forest primeval,

And the pure flower-fringed brooks.

Go to the trees and get their good tidings.

Have an autumn day in the woods, and beneath

The airy arches of limbs and leaves,

Linger in the paths of peace."

(Exit)

Epilog:

On September 4, 1915, Americans presented themselves with a gift and a promise, 358 square miles of majestic wilderness cascading from the top of the nation, the Crown Jewel of the Rockies, and a promise to keep her forever free. The efforts of many culminated on that auspicious day, but for Enos A. Mills, the preservation of this greatest of national treasures had been a personal quest spanning three decades of his life. He called a name for her, and it was *Rocky Mountain National Park*. Today we celebrate the 75th birthday of that name, and our promise, but the land itself is eternal, a legacy of antiquity. It was here before us and it will be here after us. We are but a moment in her time.

Both Choruses:

> The spirit of the park speaks to us all,
>
> Though we visit, but never remain.
>
> Someday when you least expect it
>
> You'll remember her haunting refrain.
>
> When thunder erupts in the distance,
>
> You'll recall how it rumbled there.
>
> You'll remember the swish of her sylvan skirts
>
> And the rainbows in her hair,
>
> Or a dancing brook that laughs as it goes,
>
> The thundering applause as it falls,
>
> The chatter of forests teeming with life,
>
> And the echoes of canyon walls.
>
> From the distant horizon she'll beckon
>
> And nothing will hold you then.
>
> You'll rush to the foothills, and climb to the clouds,
>
> 'Til you stand on the summit again.

#

Resources for Grand Lake Pageant, Act IV

A few very respected and influential historical figures were represented in this work. You can read more about them and their contributions to the birth and development of Rocky Mountain National Park through the following links:

http://www.foresthistory.org/publications/FHT/FHTSpringFall2007/FHT_2007_BioPortraitMills.pdf

https://archive.org/stream/aladyslifeinroc00birdgoog#page/n2/mode/2up

http://www.sierraclub.org/sierra/201207/david-brower-memories-conservation-giant-250.aspx

http://www.ghhs.us/Dunraven.htm

http://www.cr.nps.gov/history/online_books/sontag/albright.htm

http://www.nps.gov/history/history/online_books/romo/buchholtz/chap6.htm

Acknowledgements

A special thanks to those who have contributed to this work with their editing advice, photos, and encouragement.

Thanks to Carissa Allison, Cynthia Boisvert, Jenna Boisvert, Braden Lawson, Cassell Lawson, Dorcas Leonhardt, Linda Pepler, Sonya Vallejo, Abby & Shawn Warren, and Darrell Warren, whose generosity has enriched this work significantly.

Especially thank you to Ed Kallio, as I can publish nothing without his sage advice and input.

And to my P.E.O. sisters whose interest in my writing inspired this publication.

About the Author

Janice Lawson began writing poetry as a child in Texas. Her love of the artform gave her an artistic outlet for celebrating her later loves, parenting, teaching, and living in Colorado. Much of the poetry in this publication was written in and around Grand County, Colorado, the breathtakingly beautiful area that lies west of Rocky Mountain National Park.

A rich lifetime of teaching students from preschool age to college age, provided a wealth of material for many of the works included in the *Little Hearts* section of this book. Her own daughters' delightful antics provided even more.

Retired from teaching public school and courses at Colorado Mesa University, Ms. Lawson has encouraged hundreds of students to love and improve their own writing. She continues to live in Grand Junction, Colorado with her husband, Ed Kallio and canine sidekick, Lily.

She now spends her time traveling, which includes visiting her vast treasury of family and friends, and working on upcoming publications: an autobiography, *A Diary of Christmases*; and the sequel to *Kuya Kai, Adventures of an Alaskan Chow Puppy*; *On the Fly, Kijik and I*. This is her third published book to date.

Special memory: visiting Pablo Neruda's home in Valparaiso, Chile, and reading and translating poetry written in his own hand.

Many of the works in this book were previously published under the name Janice Allison. Ms. Lawson is pictured on the title page of *Silly Songs*.

Other Works by Janice Lawson

Grand County Heritage Cookbook

Out of print; Available from authors Janice Allison (Lawson) and Carole Kramer, artwork by G. Lee Boehner

Kuya Kai, the Adventures of An Alaskan Chow Puppy

Available electronically through Amazon and Barnes and Noble for Kindle and Nook e-readers and Apps.

Poems to See Me Through

Available electronically through Amazon and Barnes and Noble for Kindle and Nook e-readers and Apps.

9407532R00062

Made in the USA
San Bernardino, CA
15 March 2014